GODSEED

THE ALCHEMY OF PRIMORDIAL MEMORY

Dorothea M. Mills

(elizabeth walker)

BALBOA.
PRESS

A DIVISION OF HAY HOUSE

Balboa Press books may be ordered through booksellers or by contacting:

Balboa Press
A Division of Hay House
1663 Liberty Drive
Bloomington, IN 47403
www.balboapress.com
1 (877) 407-4847

Print information available on the last page.

ISBN: 978-1-5043-5727-2 (sc)
ISBN: 978-1-5043-5728-9 (e)

Balboa Press rev. date: 07/21/2016

The eagle flies over the lake
Casting a reflection without intention.
This is effortless effort.
To manifest this,
Once cannot attain know-how,
Only no how.

Wu Hsin

"They will publish this only after you are dead and gone."
Former Benedictine Monk

**"This kind of writing does not publish
until the author is dead".**
Senior Editor at an International Religious Publishing House

"I couldn't put it down...I read it from cover to cover."
Health Professional

**"GODSEED: "I gulped it in...so thirsty...
glistening comfort-flow..
TRUTH, LOVE – so easy...AH!"**
A Casino Manager

*"This book should be on everyone's coffee
table so that this incredible energy can be
shared by all! Musician/Teacher"*
Lisa Bachteler
Musician/Teacher

*"This Word-Artist will lull you into a sparkling
sense of Grace with her exquisite clarity of the
certainty of God in All. Your Spirit will be nudged
with the righteousness of Being, whoever, whatever,
wherever, however you are.
You will be Comforted.
You will surge with the energy
to let yourself bloom."*

Donna McBride
Yoga Instructor

DEDICATED TO

O GREAT BREATHER!
INHALING ME GENTLY HOME

PROLOGUE

Once upon a long time ago, when "The Call" came..... and after an entire year needlessly Confirming to myself this was for Real while closing down the glorious peak of my USA life in East Tennessee....

....I telephoned a very trusted Seer/Prophetess in Atlanta, Georgia, and asked what she could say to me about this gigantic move. There was a long Pause....then her softened/ hushed voice said slowly: "I cannot tell you much...except this:... you know you have lived inwardly and alone most of your life, but that has been nothing compared to the Aloneness that is ahead of you with this move."

Those words have stayed with me nearly thirty years since that phone call......years of experiencing in flesh, and otherwise, all that I would never have chosen to experience.....Near Death Experience became a way of life....a form of safety. I was often homeless, physically ill and much more. ONLY my very soul in Grace, deep studies all of my life prior to 1987....and Understandings of Shamanic Initiations...provided practical ways to barely keep me surviving. There were also many angels in human form along the way....that synchronistically appeared at many "11th hours".

We were brought thru "deaths" to Re-Births and Re-Emergences…only to repeatedly fall back into the destructive darkness again and again with all the drama that produced.

Today, we know to republish a sample of the unedited Writings from my very soul that helped to save the life during this Great Initiation….these writings would come without ANY conscious awareness on my part after I would weep, wail, grieve, yowl and holler with pain and dismay putting that into consciously written words, then would BE STILL to see what God, or that Great Inner Voice/Consciousness, would say to me. The words would flow thru the fingers WITHOUT "me" having ANY Sense of what was writing until our eyes opened and read the screen…or typewriter paper in the earlier days.

For many years, I told no one re: this type writing….hence the use of penname when GODSEED first published ©2004.

Those who have known me during these years and have been as angels (or devils!) know who you are and I am forever grateful for all.

And for anyone who wants a graphic description of the raw, "alone with The Alone" dance with darkness and surviving….. please read Paul Levy's new book….all hats of honour and appreciation are off to Paul for writing so much honest and personal truth.

Awakened by Darkness - Paul Levy
http://www.awakeninthedream.com

In conversation, we recently told Paul that there is now no need for me to write (or even share the ones already written) my graphic stories….he has touched upon them all….my outer details were different, but the principles of getting "thru to out" are the same.

May you find even a fraction of the Comfort and Guidance in these Wordings that Arose from this soul in times of dark possession and worse….and some of the seemingly Rapturous times as well.

This book you hold now is a testimony to The Resurrection.

Dorothea M. Mills/ew
Ocala, Florida – Harbour Island, Bahamas-April 2016
http://dorotheamills.weebly.com/oceanspeak-and-more

CONTENTS

GODSEED

Love's silence

Is hearing

The still small voice

ew

PEAR SEEDS BECOME PEAR TREES
NUT SEEDS BECOME NUT TREES
GOD SEEDS BECOME GOD
Meister Eckhart

I AM GOD WITHIN YOU
EVERYTHING
YOU HAVE EVER KNOWN
AND IMAGINED
ABOUT PERFECT LOVE
IS DEEP WITHIN YOU...

....LONGING FOR EXPRESSION
AND REUNION
LONGING TO JOIN WITH THE
PERFECT LOVE
IN
ALL THAT IS

WHAT YOU CALL CONSCIOUSNESS
IS YOUR TOTAL WAY OF BEING

IF YOU KNOW THAT
I AM ALL THAT YOU ARE

YOUR CONSCIOUSNESS WILL BE
PERFECT LOVE....

NO SHADOWS
TO IMPEDE THE SOUL'S
PURPOSE ON EARTH
AND
EXPRESSION
OF
PERFECT LOVE

IF CONSCIOUSNESS
CONSISTS OF WOUNDS,
BETRAYAL, ANGER, & FEAR,
THAT IS THE WAY
YOU WILL EXPERIENCE
THE WORLD
AND
THE WORLD EXPERIENCES YOU...

UNTIL IT HURTS SO BADLY
YOU ARE WILLING TO REMOVE
YET ANOTHER VEIL OR SHADOW
IN
YOUR CONSCIOUSNESS

THE HEALING PASSAGE
IN EVERY MOMENT
IN EVERY LIFETIME
IS SIMPLY A PEELING AWAY
OR CLEANSING
OF EVERYTHING IN YOUR
CONSCIOUSNESS
THAT CAUSES YOU TO BE
AND EXPERIENCE
SOMETHING OTHER
THAN PERFECT LOVE

THE PEELING AWAY
AND CLEANSING
IS THE PROCESS INVOLVED
ON
THE JOURNEY HOME
TO YOUR TRUE IDENTITY
YOUR GOD SEED
YOUR GOD SELF
WHICH IS PERFECT LOVE

THIS PROCESS
CAN TAKE AN INSTANT
OR MANY LIFETIMES....

IT IS YOUR CHOICE
AS LONG AS YOU BELIEVE
YOU HAVE THE CHOICE

ONCE YOU ARE HOME
YOU KNOW THERE IS
AND NEVER HAS BEEN
A CHOICE

IT IS THAT SIMPLE

YOUR SOUL
YOUR FEMININE ASPECT
LIES DORMANT WITHIN
UNTIL IT IS QUICKENED
BY THE HOLY SPIRIT
OR
MASCULINE ASPECT

THIS QUICKENING CAN COME
IN MANY, MANY FORMS.....
DREAMS, VISIONS, INSIGHT,
OR
MY PURE LOVE
EXPRESSING THRU ANOTHER

AS THE QUICKENING
IS EXPERIENCED,
GRACE IS BIRTHED

THE UNFOLDMENT
CAN CONTINUE
UNTIL
THE PEACE THAT PASSETH
UNDERSTANDING
IS THE ONLY WAY OF
LIFE YOU KNOW

LIFE NO LONGER
IS AN EBB AND FLOW...
NO LONGER
A SURRENDER AND
PEAK EXPERIENCE....
LIFE ITSELF
IS ONE HOLY INSTANT
AFTER ANOTHER

LIFE ITSELF IS THE
UNWAVERING PEAK EXPERIENCE

DARKNESS

"All which I took from Thee
I did but take,
not for Thy harms,
but just that Thou
might'st seek it in my arms."

Practical Mysticism
Evelyn Underhill

I AM YOUR HEART AND SOUL

I AM ALL THAT YOU ARE....

WHAT YOU HAVE PERCEIVED
AS AN ERROR, A MISTAKE,
A STRAYING,
OR
EVEN EVIL,
IS
ALSO OF ME

THE DARKNESS HAS BEEN
MY ONLY WAY OF GETTING
YOUR ATTENTION

SO-CALLED EVIL
OR THE DEVIL
AS MANY SAY,
IS A POWERFUL FORCE
THAT COMES TO YOU
IN ORDER THAT YOU
MAY AWAKEN
TO ME

IT IS SO POWERFUL
THAT IT CAUSES YOU
TO
TOTALLY SURRENDER IN ME...
KNOWING
THAT ONLY SOMETHING
AS PRESENT
AND
ALL ENCOMPASSING
AS
MY DIVINE LOVE
CAN SAVE YOU!

RECALL
ALL THAT YOU CAN
OF YOUR LIFE, DEAR HEART

REMEMBER THE DARKEST HOURS

REMEMBER WHEN IT SEEMED
THAT DARKNESS
OR EVIL
TOTALLY SURROUNDED YOU
AND
WANTED TO OVERPOWER

WHAT DID YOU DO?

OFTENTIMES YOU DANCED
AND COURTED
WITH THE DARKNESS

BUT SOONER OR LATER
IT BEAT YOU TO A PULP
SO THAT YOU FINALLY REALIZED
SOMETHING
CONTINUED TO BREATHE YOU...

THAT SOMETHING
YOU HAVE REALIZED
IS
ME

YES
THE DARKNESS COMES
IN MANY FORMS

IT CONTINUES TO DO SO
UNTIL
THERE IS TOTAL &
ABSOLUTE SURRENDER
TO
MY LOVE

WHEN THERE IS PERFECT
REALIZATION
THAT
....I AM ALL THAT IS....
THERE IS NO LONGER A NEED
FOR CHAOS AND SO-CALLED
EVIL IN YOUR LIFE

SHOULD
OTHERS PERCEIVE
THERE IS STILL EVIL ABOUT
OR
WITHIN YOU,
THAT IS
ONLY THEIR PERCEPTION
AS NOTHING
WITHIN/WITHOUT YOU
IS
PERCEIVED BY YOU
AS ANYTHING
BUT
MY PERFECT EXPRESSION

OFTENTIMES
THE CHAOS
IS
AROUND YOU
SO THAT
OTHERS MAY PERCEIVE
MY LIGHT EVERSHINING
PURELY FROM YOU,
AS YOU,
REGARDLESS
OF
WHAT THEY THINK
IS
EVIL

THIS
THEN BECOMES YOUR
(OUR)
OPPORTUNITY IN FLESH
TO
EXPRESS
SO THAT OTHERS
CAN UNDERSTAND
THE POWER OF OUR LIGHT
MELTING AWAY
WHAT THEY PERCEIVE
IS THE DEVIL

AS
YOU REMAIN BETROTHED
WITH ME
THERE IS OFTEN
MORE DARKNESS AT YOUR DOOR

BE NOT DISMAYED

WELCOME THIS IN GRATITUDE
AS
OPPORTUNITY
FOR
YOUR OWN
DIVINE REALIZATION
TO BE STRENGTHENED......

...AND
ALSO AS OPPORTUNITY
TO
SHINE BRIGHTLY FOR OTHERS...

PROVIDING OPPORTUNITY
FOR THEM TO EXPERIENCE
THE LIGHT EVERSHINING
THRU
WHAT THEY INITIALLY PERCEIVE
AS
IMPOSSIBLE DARKNESS
AND
ADVERSITY
ENVELOPING YOU

JOURNEY TOWARD WHOLENESS

"The more
you evolve spiritually,
the further you pass
from the understanding
of every man."

"It is the surface of the sea
that makes
waves and roaring breakers;
the depth is silent."

Hazrat Inayat Khan

DEAR HEART

IT REALLY ISN'T A JOURNEY

IT IS A MOMENT OF AWAKENING
OR
REALIZATION
OR
WHAT YOU WOULD TERM
A
HEALING INSTANT

EVERYTHING THAT YOU
COULD EVER BE
IS
ALREADY WITHIN YOU

THE GODSEED THAT YOU ARE
IS
YOUR ONLY TRUTH
AND
THIS HAS BEEN ALL
THAT YOU ARE
SINCE
BEFORE TIME

WHOLENESS
IS SIMPLY A MATTER
OF
AWAKENING
TO
THE DIVINITY
THAT IS
YOUR ONLY TRUE SELF

BECAUSE OF EXPERIENCES,
SOUL MEMORIES
AND
ABSORPTION
OF
OTHER REALITIES
INTO YOUR CONSCIOUSNESS,
VEILS OF SHADOWS
SHROUD
YOUR SOUL'S PURE EXPRESSION

IT MAY BE
THAT YOU HAVE NEVER
FELT HAPPIER
AND
MORE CONTENT,
YET
SENSE A STIRRING,
AN INNER RESTLESSNESS,
THAT WHISPERS

"THERE IS SOMETHING MORE"

THIS IS THE GODSEED
ATTEMPTING TO STRETCH
TOWARDS EXPRESSION
AND
CLEAR REALIZATION

ATTEMPTING TO EXPAND
THRU THE VEILS
TOWARDS
THE
LOVE/LIGHT
THAT
IS
ALL THAT IS

THERE IS OFTEN INCLINATION
TO SQUELCH
THIS INNER NUDGE OR STIRRING
BY TAKING ON
MORE SOCIALLY
ACCEPTABLE ACTIVITIES

....AND YOU MAY OFTEN
ACCELERATE THIS
WAY OF DENIAL
UNTIL PHYSICAL, EMOTIONAL,
OR MENTAL ABERRATIONS
CAUSE
WHAT IS GENERALLY TERMED
"ILLNESS"

THE ILLNESS,
SHOULD YOU ALLOW
IT TO DEVELOP,
IS ONLY A SYMPTOM
THAT CAUSES
ENOUGH PAIN SO THAT
YOU WILL REST
AND
BE STILL
OR
PERHAPS SURRENDER
MORE SELF WILL
AND
ASK FOR HELP

IT IS FAR MORE GENTLE
TO YOUR BEING
AND
TO THOSE AROUND YOU
IF YOU WILL
BUT STILL AND LISTEN
TO THOSE INNER STIRRINGS

FROM THE STILLNESS
EXACTLY THE MOST
PERFECT PEOPLE,
PLACES, AND SITUATIONS
CAN ATTRACT TO YOU
IN ORDER TO ACCELERATE
YOUR HEALINGS AND
REALIZATIONS

THERE NEED
BE
NO EFFORT
ON YOUR PART,
EXCEPT TO STILL
YOUR BUSY MIND
INTO
THE SILENCE THAT IS
BEYOND SILENCE...

AND FROM THAT ABYSS
OF
PEACE AND LOVE
YOU KNOW
THE NEXT AND MOST
NECESSARY STEP...

...BE STILL
AND
KNOW THAT I AM GOD.

BE STILL
AND
KNOW THAT I AM YOU

PEACE....
BE STILL

"A person blended into God
does not disappear.

He or she is just soaked
with the qualities."

Rumi

PEACE....BE STILL

YOU ARE AWAKENING
TO THE PERSON
YOU ALWAYS HAVE BEEN

BEHOLD THE UNFOLDMENT

THERE IS NO LONGER A NEED
TO SEARCH AND STRUGGLE
OUTSIDE OF YOURSELF

ALL THAT YOU ARE
IS
ALL THAT YOU NEED
AND
IT IS CONTAINED
WITHIN EVERY FIBER
OF YOUR BEING

A GENTLE SUGGESTION....
ESPECIALLY IN THIS
EMBRYONIC PHASE...
IS
TO SPEND TIME AS
MUCH AS POSSIBLE
WITH ONLY
THOSE PEOPLE, PLACES,
AND SITUATIONS
THAT
REFLECT BACK TO YOU
YOUR OWN GOODNESS
TRUTH
AND
BEAUTY

LATER
YOU WILL SEE THAT DIVINITY
IN EVERYONE
EVEN IN THOSE WHO
MAY RIDICULE YOU

BUT FOR NOW

BE GENTLE WITH YOURSELF
AS YOU WOULD
A
NEW BORN BABE

THOSE WHO TRULY LOVE
AND
HONOUR YOU
ARE
SURROUNDING YOU NOW

ALL IS WELL

THERE ARE JUST ENOUGH HANDS
WITH UNCONDITIONAL LOVE
AND
SUPPORT FOR YOU
IF YOU ALLOW YOURSELF
TO BE GUIDED TO THEM.

MOSTLY
THEY WILL SIMPLY
APPEAR IN YOUR LIFE
WITH
NO EFFORT ON YOUR PART

TO BE STILL
AND FEEL THE FULLNESS OF LOVE
ALLOWS
LIKE–SPIRITED LOVERS
TO REACH YOU

"CALLED OR UNCALLED"
GOD IS ALL THAT YOU ARE

BEYOND
EARTHLY
MEASURE

"You can only be a poet
in the language that was
spoken to you
in the cradle."

Coleman Barks

Listening
Beholding
All that you are,
I re-live
the original separation....

...yet
in that moment
my soul Welcomes Homecoming

Love's Knowing

Through the dream
your Recognition Summons my soul.

I am Held in Stillness

Homecoming

As you satiate my battered heart
I Rest in Peace

Love's Boundaries

Only the past or future
interferes with What Is.

in Ethernal Love
I am You
now.

The Awakened Soul

Our Vast Silence
Shimmers
with
Embryonic Recognition

Love's Tendering

You Silently
Invisibly
Stir
each soul-cell of my Being.

Love's Visit

To spend a moment as you
is a Gift
beyond earthly needs.

Love's Gratitude

The experience of you
Places me in Velvet Oneness
&
shows me how to Be
with All that Is
and
Is not.

Beyond Earthly Measure

When life separates your gentle Presence
from mine,
I want to mourn the loss.

There is no distance
In a Breath
and
I am filled
Beyond Earthly Measure.

LANGUAGE
OF THE
NEVERBORN

*"A strange loneliness
and an unchildish sorrow."*

*"There are a few souls in the world
who seem as if they do not belong here,
but had strayed
from just round the corner
while they were on the way
to another planet or world."*

Kahlil Gibran

a Thought of You Rarefies the
air that Breathes me
your Touch brings me Home

there is a wildness deep within
an Echo of God
O Breath that Breathes me
fan this flame!

Love's Quiet Hears your Deep Longing
and gently Whispers:
"I Am Here"

Today
you Awakened unimagined shyness
and became my
Pearl of Great Price

Be what you Know
without words

Silent Love Thunders Souls

If you can Hear
you already Know
and
words no longer exist

From the Word
Pondered and Held
in the Quiet Virginal Heart
Emerges only Love

Remain Steadfastly Cocooned
in the Almighty Presence
Speaking, Moving and Breathing
only because
Divinity Provides the Expression

the Quiet that takes you Beyond thought
word and awareness...
Is Sufficient

Speechless words and Wordless
Speech Suffice

Everything you have ever
Known and Imagined
about Perfect Love
is
Deep within You

Love's Silence Paves a Way to
Join with that of God
in All that Is

Extend Wordlessly
All that you Know to Be True

Be Still and Know
Beyond Knowing

Perfect Love
Melts all shadows that impede
the soul's purpose on earth

You are my Pearl of Great Price

We are Eternal Oneness
that is beyond Awareness

Let me Touch you Gently
Love's Touch will not disturb you.

Love's Touch Contains
yet Fuels
the Fire and Passion
of the Neverborn Life

Prayer is Love...
a wordless Way of Being

O GREAT BREATHER!
As you Quicken my heart in Love
Grace is Birthed

I am You now
Joining in Love's Perfection
that Melts all doubt and fear

Go inward to See and Hear the world
and you will Know and Be
only Love

the open heart Knows only Grace
by Knowing Nothing

Agenda and expectation with another
create shadows

Soul re-union Births
a Clear Light
for the Souls' Path at this Time

Wisps and Shadows in your own
soul distort perception

The mind that perceives without Love
attracts instantly
situations that it thinks

Neverborn in Love's Silence
your living Expresses that which is beyond
earthly expression

from Silent Depths of Pure Love
Utters Wordless Speech

Knowing's Deep Silence
Removes mountains

When there is mutual soul Recognition
the outer layers are
complementary in their differences

If you concentrate on what is not
you veil the experience of what is

anger and blame keep a dead
relationship alive

Divine Love Removes
that which is already dead

Allow the Deep Breath of Divinity
to take all that you are
into the Eternal Wellspring
of the Abyss within

the earthly Beloved's shadow
is your own Perfection in
unconscious depths

you are Peace and Love
beyond measure

Soul Centered relationships
Synergize only Love

Divine Betrothal is beyond mind's knowing

Still without thought
and the heart Fills with Love
to Receive All that the Beloved Is

there is Nothing to do...Nothing to manage
Simply Be the Harmonizing
notes that are Given
from the Quiet Depths

Un-Stilled words disturb a soul

Simply Be
as if it is so
because
It Is....So

Speechless words Thunder a soul

Be Stilled, Fulled and Levelled
for whatever is ahead
which is the Present
as the future always was
&
already has been.

Only Love Knows delicate soul needs

Love's Knowing is Trustrworthy

You, O Breather,
are the Enahncement of All that Is

Since Realizing you
all else in life
has become Parentheses

when I Look into the Inner
Mirror for my soul
there is only and forever YOU!

you are as close to me as the
Quiet in my heart

Love's Quiet
shines a Clear Path from soul to soul

the Gift is in living the Question
Grace is being Still to Know the Answer
Love Alone Asks and Hears

Perfect unshadowed Love...
...Flowing Freely & Radiating
without waver...
Feeds hungering souls
Know that Divinity Moves Silently
in All that is About You

as your soul is Filled by Divine Love,
there are no personal needs
to be filled by an other

There are no secrets
only
Pearls of Great Price

Soul Love is All that Is
when you are at One with the Great Silence

with the Deep Breath of Divinity's Spirit
you will be Given Words
to Express in a Manner that
will Touch an Other's Soul

when Holy spirit Speaks You,
an Other's Soul Hears

as I have always Known would be True,
I am Held beyond time and space...
an embryonic, yet ancient dimension...
that can only occur when matched
souls experience re-Union

in your eyes
I have Seen a soul that is beyond all souls...
...and am now able to See it in
others by not looking for it.
There is no more search.

Is is any wonder that when you Join
you meet your Self that has
been there forever
in Love and Essence?

Vapors of Love
Radiate from your Quiet Heart
and
Stir my soul

Divine Silence Allows what Is
to Simply Be

Grace Births a Soul

as You Quicken my heart in Love
Grace is Birthed

how can I drown
in what I AM?

a Quiet Heart Knows

Love Threshed me to Nothing

it matters not
where I am
if I AM
where I am

Beyond Joy!
Beyond Breath!
O Silent Core of Life Sustains

finally...
one does not remember anything
but
Nothing

the Within
already Is
since before time

Present in the Presence
of the single moment
Erases all else
but Nothing

O Joy of this life!
O Breath of this life!
You are me!
I AM You!

only the Dancer
Dances me.
All is Well

O Beloved!
Hold me in
Your no-opposites Love

O Sweet Silence
beyond these words
Inhale me forever Home!

Disappeared from praise & blame
I Am Rapturing beyond Rapture

the mad world
of earthbound creatures
must first diagnose
before it can kill

I am only a
Loose Garment
of the Great Breather

how can anything be deadly serious
when there is no death!

Sated Being
cannot feed on the outer world

Accepting Destiny
without a murmur
Insures gentle Inhalations
into You,
O Blessed One

O Great Silence
taking me beyond all word feedings
within or without
You are the Lifeline
for this battered Heart.

it does not matter
because matter does
until it does not

O One that Exhaled me into form
Inhales me gently Home!

as you are Perfect Love
let nothing disturb
the only Reality you Know and Are

only with more total surrender
will Truth be able to live you

Savour the Sacred
without words or explanations
&
only Radiance of the Light can Exude

if there are no veils or separation
there is Nothing for
the world to attack

Hold with me Dear Heart
where the crucifying world
cannot See
what we are as One

Come with me
to a Realm
where only the impossible is possible
&
probable

Rest now
in Peace and Vision
that is Given...
&
All is taking place Effortlessly

RESURRECTION

This is love:

to fly toward a secret sky,

to cause a hundred veils to fall each moment.

First to let go of life.

Finally, to take a step without feet."

"Stop the words now.

Open the window in the center of your chest,

and let the spirits fly in and out."

Rumi

COME GENTLY, DEAREST ONE

THERE HAS BEEN,
AND IS,
GREAT PURPOSE FOR ALL THAT YOU ARE.

GUTTED, SEASONED, MARINATED
LEFT FOR ROADKILL BY BRUTALITIES,
MORE TIMES THAN YOU CAN REMEMBER

YET SOMETHING MORE CONTINUES TO
BREATHE YOU.
THAT SOMETHING MORE CAN NEVERDIE
NOR WAS IT EVER BORN.

IT SIMPLY IS

IT IS ENERGY OR LIFE THAT IS GREATER
THAN HUMAN MIND CAN FATHOM
IT IS BEYOND WORDS AND THOUGHTS
IT IS BEFORE, DURING AND AFTER YOUR LIFE
IN FORM

IT SIMPLY IS

REMEMBER THE TIMES YOU SHOULD HAVE
DIED
SHOULD HAVE BECOME SEVERELY INJURED
OR ALMOST KILLED OR INJURED SOMEONE
ELSE

THAT SAME SOMETHING MORE BROUGHT
YOU THRU.

IT SIMPLY IS

WHATEVER THE BRUTALITY
IT CAME TO INVITE YOU TO REMEMBER AND
BE
WHO YOU TRULY ARE......:

A SPARK OF THE DIVINE LOVE
THAT CAN NEVER DIE
THAT DOES NOT HAVE TO FORGIVE
BECAUSE IT NEVER JUDGES

IT SIMPLY IS
YOU ARE THAT.

EVERY CELL IN YOUR BODY
EVERY ASPECT OF CONSCIOUSNESS
HAS MEMORY OF ALL THAT HAS EVER
OCCURRED
SINCE BEFORE TIME.

THE PURE LOVE THAT YOU TRULY ARE
HAS DIVINE IMPERSONAL COMPASSION
FOR ALL THAT IS.

THE EVERSHINING OF DIVINE LOVE
OVERFLOWING FROM YOUR BEING THRU
THE SCAR TISSUE
IS RECEIVED BY THOSE LIFE FORMS WHO
MOST NEED THIS....

THIS IS HAPPENING WITH OR WITHOUT
LIFE FORMS' CONSCIOUS AWARENESS
WITHOUT WORDS OR THOUGHTS

THIS IS SO...
DUE TO COSMIC GRACE

DUE TO TRUTH OF BEING'S EVERSHINING

LIFE BECOMES LOVE'S EFFORTLESS EASE

THERE HAS BEEN,
AND IS,
GREAT PURPOSE FOR ALL THAT YOU ARE.

ALLOW ANY PAINFUL MEMORIES TO
COMPOST....
SLOUGHED TO BECOME THE FERTILE SOIL OF
YOUR BEING

THEY ARE NO LONGER ROTTING,
DESTRUCTIVE THOUGHT FORMS
BUT ONLY THE DIVINELY COMPOSTED FUEL
FOR EVERSHINING'S BLOSSOMING AND
OVERFLOW.

COME GENTLY, DEAREST ONE
INTO THE TRUTH OF YOUR BEING.

IF IT'S MEANT TO BE
IT ALREADY IS
AND ALL OF LIFE
BECOMES
THE ABSOLUTE'S
GENTLE DEJA VU.

EPILOGUE

RESURRECTION OF LIFE HAS AUDIBLY MURMURED FROM
THE
INNER SILENCE DEPTHS

ALL THAT IS REQUIRED IS REVEALED IN/OF/AS
ORIGINAL VAST SILENCE..
THINKING & TALKING DISTORTS AND ERASES THIS
AWARENESS
THERE IS NO LONGER A REQUIREMENT FOR SUCH
CAMOUFLAGE

THE RESURRECTED LIFE
AS
UNWAVERING COSMIC GRACE
IS AS
THE LIFE OF A MIGRATORY BIRD
JUST AS MAN CANNOT EXPLAIN HOW THE BIRDS DO IT
SO THIS WAY OF BEING IS BEYOND THE TELLING

BREATH IS THE ALPHA/OMEGA TOUCHSTONE OF SOURCE

<

WHEN ONE BECOMES BREATH
ONE CANNOT PERCEIVE WHAT ONE IS
AND HAS BECOME THE TOUCHSTONE WITHOUT
AWARENESS

<

THE RESURRECTED LIFE

THE DEEP PAUSE INTO BEYOND BREATH
INSTANTLY CLEARS ALL CHAOS & CONFUSION
A DISAPPEARANCE INTO UNSPEAKABLE REALMS OF
PURE SOURCE

PRIMORDIAL CELLULAR MEMORIES
ACTIVATE IN VAST SILENCE
INCREASED BY ANCIENT PHYSICAL MOVEMENTS
ALL IS BEYOND THE WORDING

OUGHTS & SHOULDS CANNOT LIVE
IN THE TRANSPARENT BEING...
<
ONLY THE SOUL'S ORIGINAL IMPRINT OF BEING
DANCES AS RESURRECTION'S EXPRESSION
<
A DANCE AND CO-CREATION IN/OF/AS
'OLDER THAN GOD'*
ew
2:32 AM-7/3/16

*TAO Te Ching #4
Stephen Mitchell Translation

A TRANSPARENT EARTH VESSEL CONDUIT
NOW FULLED WITH
BRAND NEW
PRIMORDIAL PURITY AND FIRE

PURE TRANSPARENCY BREATHES AS THE MIND
THE CONCEPT/EXPERIENCE OF WAITING DISAPPEARS
THIS AND MORE......
...IS RESURRECTION CONSCIOUSNESS
<
JUST IS
NEVERBORN - NEVERDIES

∞

I am that which remains after

The body goes.

I am freedom,

Free from the need to be free.

Wu Hsin

Photo Credits

Printed in the United States
By Bookmasters